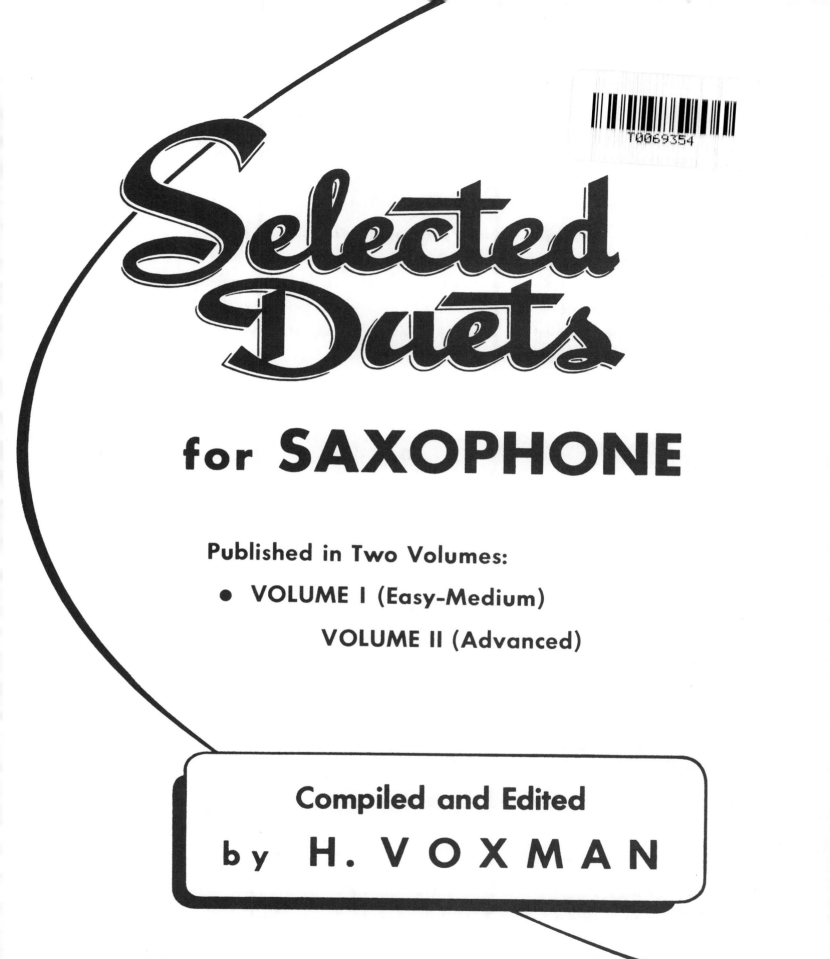

Selected Duets

for SAXOPHONE

Published in Two Volumes:

- **VOLUME I (Easy-Medium)**

  VOLUME II (Advanced)

Compiled and Edited

by H. VOXMAN

HAL•LEONARD®
CORPORATION

7777 W. BLUEMOUND RD. P.O. BOX 13819 MILWAUKEE, WI 53213

T0069354

Preface

Duet playing affords the student the most intimate form of ensemble experience. The problems of technic, tone quality, intonation, and ensemble balance are brought into the sharpest relief. Careful attention must be given to style as indicated by the printed page and as demanded by the intangibles of good taste.

Mastery of the art of duet playing leads easily and naturally to competent performance in the larger ensembles. The numerous works included in this volume have been selected for the purpose of introducing the saxophonist to the finest in two-part ensemble literature and acquainting him with a diversity of musical forms and expressions.

H. Voxman

●

Air

18th Century

© Copyright MCMLVIII by Rubank, Inc., Chicago, Ill.
International Copyright Secured

BERNARDS

Canzonetta

BERNARDS

Andante con moto

3

Winter

BENDER

Spring

BENDER

Autumn

BENDER

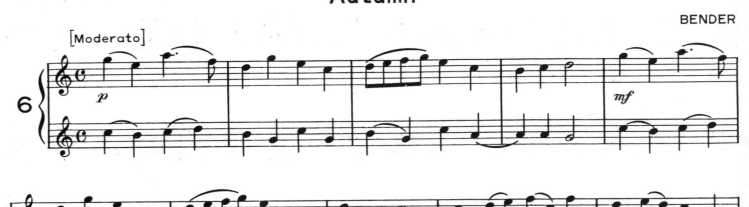

J. AUBERT

Quick Dance

PURCELL

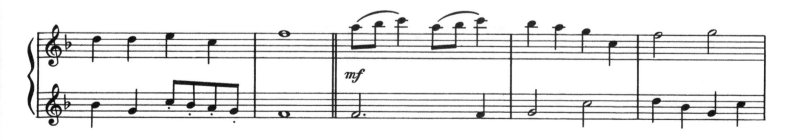

GOEDICKE

Moderato

9

Folk Song

Lively

10

Time Study

HAAG

12

Italian Rustic Dance

[Lively]

18th Century

13

Bourrée

ECCLES

14

Gigue

KING

15

Seven Exercises in Syncopation

DEVIENNE

16

17

18

Menuett

CORELLI

Allegretto

23

Duett

HASSE

Moderato

24

Minuet

18th Century

Sonata

18th Century

Allegro

Menuett

PURCELL

BOISMORTIER

BERBIGUIER

29

BENDER

30

Allegro con spirito

31

Allegro

32

Sarabande

CORELLI

33

Minuetto

HOFFMEISTER

KALLIWODA

35

37

38 [Allegretto]

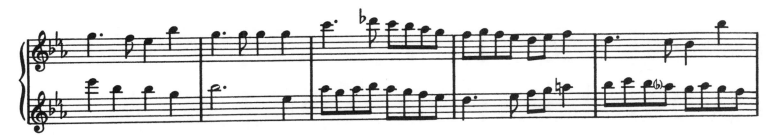

Pastorale

KRANZ

Tamburin

N. CHÉDEVILLE

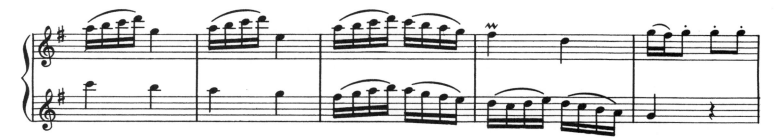

Sarabanda
(from Sonata IV)

LOEILLET

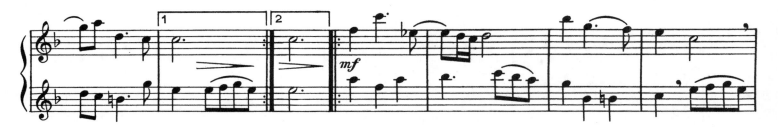

Largo

HANDEL

Marche

CAMPAGNOLI

Minor Study

CAMPAGNOLI

Menuetto

HAYDN

45

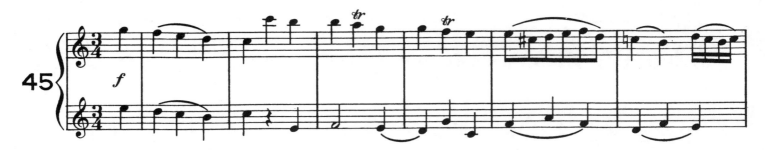

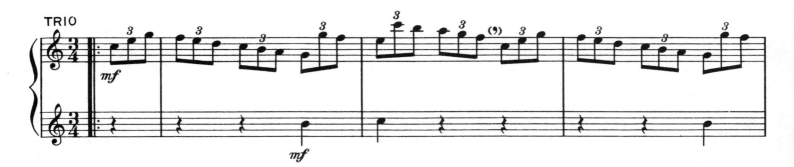

TRIO

Menuetto D. C.

PLEYEL

Andante

46

Duettino VIII

HOOK

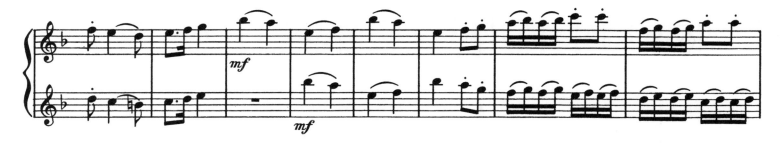

Andante con moto
CAMPAGNOLI

48

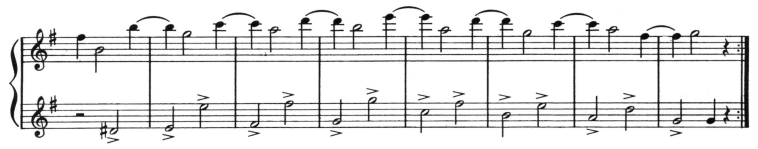

Menuetto

49

Fine

TRIO

Air

HANDEL

50

E. KOHLER

HOFFMEISTER

52

Menuetto

C. STAMITZ

53

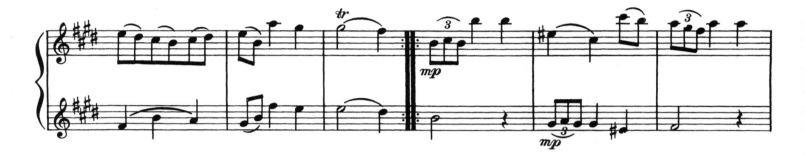

54

Fugato

STAMITZ

55

Romance

C. STAMITZ

D. C. al Fine

ROSSARI

Poco agitato

57

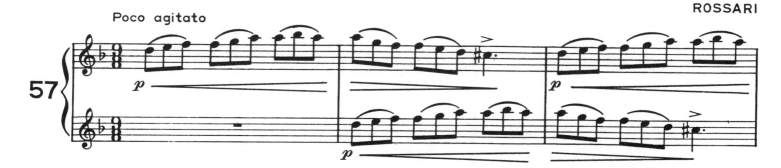

Andante con moto

58

Slow Air

FINGER

59

46

Rondo

KUMMER

KUMMER

61

Poco adagio

*

Moderato

Folk Song

63

Allemande

PURCELL

Largo [in three]

18th Century

67

Canon

W. F. BACH

Gigue

BOISMORTIER

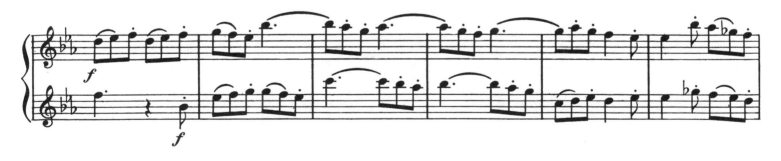

Torneo
(Turning Dance)

HAAG

WEIDEMANN

Polonaise

HAAG

Allemande

BOISMORTIER

Allegro moderato

73

NOLINSKY

Energetically

74

Hornpipe a l'Inglese

GALLIARD

MAGNANI

Allegretto tranquillo

76

DEVIENNE

77

Étude Mélodique

H. KLOSÉ

78

CAMPAGNOLI

79

FIVE DUETS

COMBELLE

Duo Concertant

COMBELLE

81

Duo Récréatif

COMBELLE

82

Duo Concertant
(Canon)

COMBELLE

83

Thème Varié

COMBELLE

Mouv^t de mazurka un peu lent

VARIATION I

VARIATION II

VARIATION III